Irmgard Lucht

THE RED POPPY

Tell me about life,
tell me about the red poppy.

—For Georgi

THE RED POPPY

IRMGARD LUCHT

HYPERION BOOKS FOR CHILDREN
NEW YORK

Summer is a green time.
Far and wide, the countryside is green.
The trees and the fields are green,
as are the meadows and the forests.
The farmer has tilled the fields
so that everything can grow.
What will grow in the fields and
the meadows will feed people and animals.

The wind sweeps over the rye field and bends the countless stalks.
Almost every seed the farmer has sown has grown into a plant.
Each plant has roots, leaves, and a stalk.
Each stalk has an ear.
The ears bear fruit—grain, the fruit of cereal plants;
grain for flour and for bread and for the seeds of new plants.

The stalks of rye grow tall and
stand close together, like a forest.
Other plants grow on the edge
of the field as well.
No one planted them;
they just grow there, wild.
Beautiful violet pansies and red poppies
grow and bloom, spots of color
in the green field.

The poppy buds droop as if wilted,
but it only looks that way.
They are waiting.
During the night,
strength flows into the delicate stems.
They stand up straight as the flowers struggle
to free themselves from the sepals.
The sepals are the green leaflike parts that
protect the bud while it develops.

The folded blossom is strong,
and it struggles out of the sepals' tight wrap.
It no longer needs protection.
Without anyone noticing,
a small miracle has happened.
The bud has given birth to a flower.
The petals are still crumpled and
nearly closed, but when they open
they will be as shining and beautiful as silk.
The four petals surrounding the flower's
center will stretch out in the sunshine.

Finally, the poppy has blossomed.
The flower opens up wide to attract visitors.
Insects are drawn by the flaming red color,
for color is the language of flowers.
Hungry insects will eat the poppy's pollen.
The pollen will also cling to their bodies
as they travel from flower to flower,
searching for food.
Some of it may fall into the blossom's heart.

The blossom's heart is the pistil.
Surrounding it, in a tight garland,
are many stamens.
Growing on the stamens is powdery pollen.
Pollen is more than just food for insects—
it is life-giving dust.
Only a little needs to get inside the pistil
in order for new seeds to grow.
Although each poppy makes its own,
it must get pollen from another poppy
in order to grow new seeds.
For that, it needs the help of insects.

For one summer's day,
a day of sun and wind and
perhaps a shower of rain,
the poppy bloomed.
On that one day it was visited by
flies, beetles, and bumblebees.
The pistil, now fertilized with pollen,
swells to become the capsule that will hold
seeds for new poppy plants.
The flower's shimmering petals wilt,
no longer needed.
The fly passes it by,
looking for nourishment elsewhere.
But what remains is what is most important:
the small green capsule.
In it, the new poppy seeds are growing.

Days of sun and rain alternate
as summer draws to an end.
Where flowers once bloomed,
grain and fruit now ripen.
The poppies are ripe, too;
their capsules are large.
As they sway in the breeze,
they drop dark tiny grains—
the poppy seeds—onto the ground.
Although each seed is smaller
than a grain of sand,
it contains the life of a new poppy.
When spring comes again,
poppy plants will grow where the seeds fell,
and in the summer, new flowers will bloom.

Summer is also a golden time.
The fields of rye and other grain
shine brightly between
the meadows and the farmland,
as if the sun were playing hide-and-seek.
Harvesttime begins in summer and
continues into autumn.
Then winter comes and puts nature to rest.
While nature sleeps, it gathers strength.
When springtime returns,
nature adorns itself with green again
and with colorful flowers.
But only in summer will nature reveal
her most beautiful color
in the flower that blooms on
the edge of the fields:
the bright red poppy.

End Notes

■ Pages 4/5
The animals in this picture are a field hare, a field mouse, a wagtail, and a cabbage butterfly.

■ Pages 6/7
Here a whinchat has spotted a gnat, and a spider has caught a cabbage butterfly in its web. There are three other insects, too: a ladybug and a beetle, both on stalks of grain, and a wasp, sitting on a chamomile flower.

■ Pages 8/9
The poppy is not the only flower to bloom in summertime: the field pansy and the lesser bindweed (climbing up a grain stalk) bloom as well. Here, the hovering fly visits a poppy, the gnat rests on a leaf, and the shrew has caught a cricket.

The poppy bee has bitten a piece out of a poppy petal and is taking it down to a small hole in the ground. Poppy bees take good care of their young. They make a hole for each egg that they lay and line the hole with pieces of poppy petals. They then store some pollen as food and fold the flower pieces over it. To further protect the egg until it hatches, the poppy bee covers everything over with soil.

■ Pages 10/11
A beetle is sleeping on the stalk of grain over the poppy bud.

■ Pages 12/13
Now the beetle has woken up and met with another beetle.

■ Pages 16/17
Like hairy violet-green cords, the stigmata lie in a star-shaped pattern on the poppy pistil. There are tiny openings leading inside the pistil, just large enough for grains of pollen.

Perhaps an insect visited another poppy bloom earlier. Some pollen may have stuck to its body. If it falls off the insect and onto the pistil, some of it may get inside. This would be a gift to the poppy because it can't be pollinated with its own pollen.

■ Pages 14/15
A hovering fly has landed on a poppy bloom. Soon it will sit on the seed capsule and feed on the pollen, like the small black bug in the middle. The beetle on the left is waiting for its turn.

■ Pages 18/19
This is one of the many varieties of hovering flies. Although they look like wasps, they can't sting.

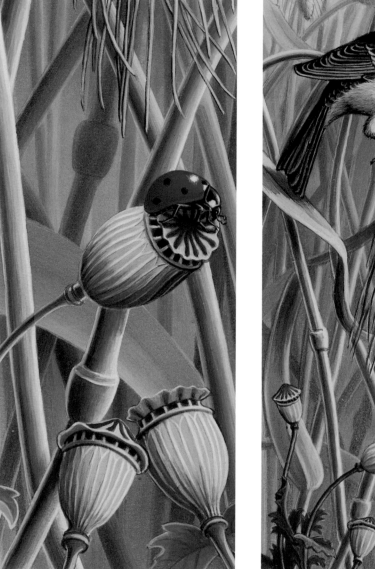  

■ Pages 20/21

Up to three thousand seeds mature within one poppy capsule. They can rest for years in the soil without anything happening. But if the soil is plowed or turned over—when a house or street is built, for example—then many of the seeds will start to sprout. Poppies can grow only in loose, aired soil.

The ladybug is sitting on the poppy capsule by chance. It doesn't eat poppy seeds. And the sparrow won't eat the ladybug. Sparrows would rather steal ripe kernels of grain.

■ Pages 22/23

Perhaps it's the gathering thunderstorm that makes the field hare run away and the partridge seek shelter. The farmer also must hurry if he wants to get his trailer full of grain home without getting it wet. But with the aid of a combine harvester, his work will soon be finished.

Author's Note

This book began with a binocular microscope, also known as a stereoscope. Unlike a microscope, it allows the viewer to see in three dimensions instead of one. Through it, one can discover the world of tiny things.

One day this instrument opened the door for me into a mysterious new world. I had just finished a series of pictures showing individual flowers greatly enlarged. But now, aided by the stereoscope, I discovered astonishing things, things hardly visible to the naked eye.

From my summer excursions outdoors, I brought back plants and flowers for my discovery trips with the stereoscope. And one day there was a poppy flower among them. I put it on the glass plate, and the light shone from below through the tender petals. My heart started throbbing. I had never seen such a fiery red color before! The enlarged seed capsule looked like a dark mysterious vessel with an elaborately decorated top. And those big strange stamens on which small beetles crawled. . . . I had to paint everything immediately. And so I started.

When at the end of that day the finished picture lay before me, I knew that what I had

discovered was so beautiful, I wanted to share it with others, with children. Of course, I can't have every child come visit me and look through the stereoscope, but I can paint what I see, and in a book I can allow others to participate.

A single picture is not enough

for a book, so I had to create others. The idea for the book came to me practically by itself when, in the following days and weeks, I went out with my bicycle and camera to look at poppy plants and photograph them. Though I prefer to use living plants as models for painting, I had to take photos for this book. Poppies bloom only during three months in summer, but this book would take a whole year to make.

The illustrations were done with acrylic paints. I use them in

a translucent glaze, putting layer upon layer over a primed white background. The white makes the colors luminous, like watercolors. And if too many layers of paint build up, I can lighten them by painting them over again with zinc white or with a mixture of white paint.

Original German language edition text and illustrations
copyright © 1994 by Ravensburger Buchverlag Otto Maier GmBh,
Postfach 1860 Marktstrasse 22–26, Ravensburg 1, D-88188, Germany.
Original German title: *Roter Mohn.*
English language text copyright © 1995 by Ravensburger Buchverlag.
First published in the United States in 1995 by Hyperion Books for Children,
114 Fifth Avenue, New York, New York 10011.
Printed in Germany.

3 5 7 9 10 8 6 4 2

Library of Congress Cataloging-in-Publication Data

Lucht, Irmgard.
[Roter Mohn. English]
The red poppy/Irmgard Lucht; [translation by Frank Jacoby-Nelson] — 1st ed.
p. cm.
ISBN 0-7868-0055-0 (trade) — 0-7868-2043-8 (lib. bdg.)
1. Poppies — Life cycles — Juvenile literature. [1. Poppies] I. Title.
QK495.P22L8313 1995 583' . 122 — dc20 94-15057 CIP AC

Translation by Frank Jacoby-Nelson.

This book is set in 18-point Garamond Light Condensed.